BUILDING BY DESIGN

ENGINEERING
THE
INTERNATIONAL
SPACE STATION

BY CECILIA PINTO MCCARTHY

CONTENT CONSULTANT
Anouck Girard
Associate Professor, Aerospace Engineering
University of Michigan

Core Library

An Imprint of Abdo Publishing
abdopublishing.com

Cover image: The International Space Station is made
up of many modules and solar arrays.

abdopublishing.com

Published by Abdo Publishing, a division of ABDO, PO Box 398166,
Minneapolis, Minnesota 55439. Copyright © 2018 by Abdo Consulting
Group, Inc. International copyrights reserved in all countries. No part of this
book may be reproduced in any form without written permission from the
publisher. Core Library™ is a trademark and logo of Abdo Publishing.

Printed in the United States of America, North Mankato, Minnesota
102017
012018

Cover Photo: NASA
Interior Photos: NASA, 1, 18; JSC/NASA, 4–5, 8, 15, 20, 23, 30, 32, 34, 36–37, 39, 43, 45; MSFC/
NASA, 12–13, 26–27

Editor: Arnold Ringstad
Imprint Designer: Maggie Villaume
Series Design Direction: Laura Polzin

Publisher's Cataloging-in-Publication Data

Names: McCarthy, Cecilia Pinto, author.
Title: Engineering the International Space Station / by Cecilia Pinto McCarthy.
Description: Minneapolis, Minnesota : Abdo Publishing, 2018. | Series: Building by design | Includes
         online resources and index.
Identifiers: LCCN 2017946983 | ISBN 9781532113727 (lib.bdg.) | ISBN 9781532152603 (ebook)
Subjects: LCSH: Space stations--Juvenile literature. | Aerospace engineering--Juvenile literature. |
         Large space structures (Astronautics)--Juvenile literature.
Classification: DDC 629.442--dc23
LC record available at https://lccn.loc.gov/2017946983

CONTENTS

CHAPTER ONE

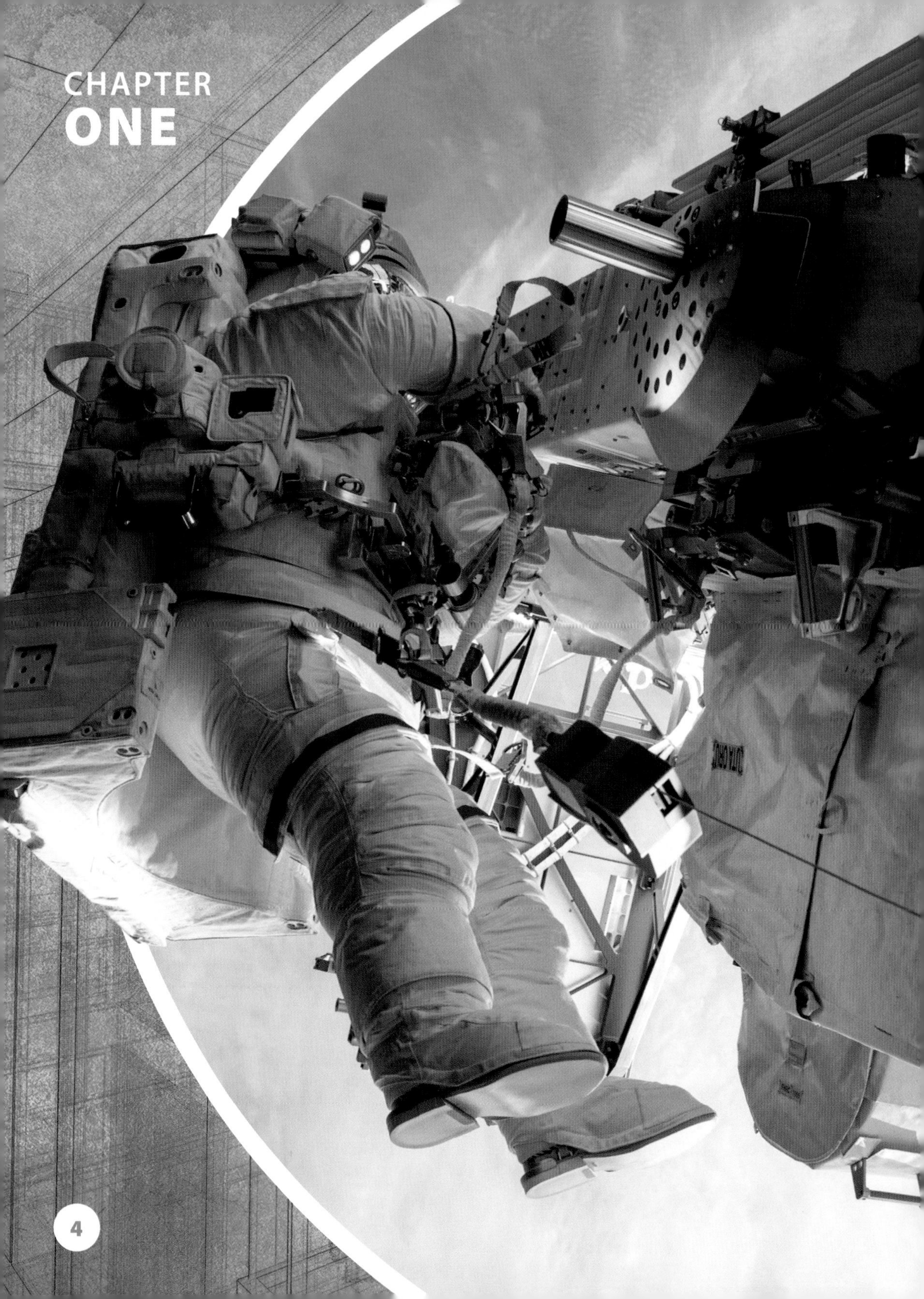

LIFE IN SPACE

On May 23, 2017, Commander Peggy Whitson opened the outer door of the Quest airlock. Fellow astronaut Jack Fischer accompanied her. They left the International Space Station (ISS). They floated out into space. Strong cables kept both astronauts tethered to the station.

This was Commander Whitson's tenth space walk, or extravehicular activity (EVA). Her task was to replace a broken computer. For almost three hours, the two astronauts worked outside the station. They were circling the planet at 17,500 miles per hour (28,000 km/h).

Whitson works on equipment outside the ISS.

BECOMING AN ISS ASTRONAUT

Astronaut candidates must have a college degree in engineering, science, or math. They complete years of tough physical and mental preparation. Training includes water survival and aircraft flight skills. They must learn Russian. Candidates learn how to put on bulky space suits. Spacewalk practice takes place in the Neutral Buoyancy Laboratory. It is the world's largest indoor pool. Candidates wear suits that keep them stable in the water. The pool mimics conditions in microgravity. Candidates practice moving around and doing repairs. After being accepted, astronauts learn specific mission skills. They learn to repair equipment and conduct experiments.

Despite this extreme speed, they heard only their radios and the whirring of air circulating in their space suits. The vivid blue and green Earth rotated below them. The inky blackness of deep space loomed above. Commander Whitson used bolts to secure the new computer. On another part of the ISS, Fischer installed two antennae. The astronauts completed their jobs. They returned to the airlock and re-entered the ISS.

THE FIRST SPACE STATIONS

In the 1970s, both the Soviet Union and the United States built space stations. The Soviet Union's cylinder-shaped Salyut stations were the first. The earliest Salyut station went into space in 1971. Solar panels collected the sun's energy for power. Cosmonauts traveled to Salyut on Soyuz spacecraft.

America's Skylab station launched in 1973. Three crews visited it. The first lived on Skylab for 28 days. Salyut and Skylab were not permanent stations. When objects orbit near Earth, their orbits gradually get lower and lower. They eventually dip into the atmosphere. Without heat shielding, they burn up. Once their missions ended and astronauts left, these early stations burned up in the atmosphere.

A PERMANENT SPACE STATION

In 1986 the Soviet Union launched a space station called Mir. It was designed to stay in space for many years. Mir had separate sections called modules. Astronauts from

Skylab was made up of a single large module.

several countries visited Mir. They conducted research. They learned about living and working in space.

In the 1980s, President Ronald Reagan approved the construction of a permanent space station. He invited other nations to join the project. At first, the plan got off to a good start. Canada, Japan, and the European Space Agency (ESA) agreed to contribute to the station. But the cost kept growing. To cut costs, the station was redesigned. Construction was delayed many years. In 1991 the Soviet Union broke up into many separate countries. The largest was Russia. It took over the Soviet space program. In 1993 Russia joined the space station effort. The project was named the International Space Station.

PERSPECTIVES

CITIZENS AGAINST THE ISS

Not everyone was happy with the construction of the ISS. In 1997 a group called the Council for Citizens Against Government Waste (CCAGW) argued that the ISS was too expensive. At the time, the ISS program cost $1.8 billion per year. Funding it took money away from other space programs. Other spacecraft were cancelled. CCAGW pointed out that the United States was already heavily in debt. It believed that money should be spent to reduce the debt rather than fund the ISS.

AN INTERNATIONAL ENGINEERING EFFORT

The ISS is a complex feat of engineering. It is the largest structure ever built in space. Most of the ISS is made up of bus-sized modules. The station is 357 feet (109 m) across. It is 290 feet (88 m) long. It weighs 925,000 pounds (420,000 kg). The station can house six or more people. It orbits Earth every 90 minutes.

The ISS is an orbiting science laboratory. Orbiting objects are in a continuous free fall. This condition is called microgravity. Microgravity allows ISS astronauts to conduct unique experiments. They observe how microgravity affects the human body. They test how it impacts plants and animals too. Their discoveries improve medical treatments and lead to new technologies. Researchers are also learning about the universe. In the future, astronauts will venture farther into space. These journeys will be made possible by the work done at the ISS.

STRAIGHT TO THE
SOURCE

In his State of the Union Address on January 25, 1984, President Ronald Reagan announced his desire for the National Aeronautics and Space Administration (NASA) to build a space station:

We can follow our dreams to distant stars, living and working in space for peaceful, economic, and scientific gain. Tonight, I am directing NASA to develop a permanently manned space station and to do it within a decade.

A space station will permit . . . leaps in our research in science, communications, in metals, and in lifesaving medicines which could be manufactured only in space. We want our friends to help us meet these challenges. . . . NASA will invite other countries to participate so we can strengthen peace, build prosperity, and expand freedom for all who share our goals.

Source: Ronald Reagan. "Address Before a Joint Session of the Congress on the State of the Union—January 25, 1984." *The American Presidency Project*. University of California, Santa Barbara, 2017. Web. Accessed May 2, 2017.

What's the Big Idea?

Take a close look at this passage. How does President Reagan feel about space exploration? What details support his point?

DESIGNING THE STATION

In 1994 the plans for the ISS began to take shape. Engineers used existing Russian and American space technologies. The Russians would build the first module. They would also be responsible for several other modules, solar panels, and other systems. The United States provided more modules and pieces of the station's structure. Canada's job was to produce a robotic arm. The Japanese engineered another robotic arm. They also designed two modules and a platform for

Early artists' renderings showed the initial plans for the ISS.

experiments. Countries of the ESA would construct the Columbus module. It would be used for microgravity research. It also developed the Automated Transfer Vehicle (ATV). This remote-controlled spacecraft would fly supplies to the ISS. When finished, the ISS would have 15 large modules and hundreds of other parts.

STRONG SHAPES

The modules had to be small enough to fit inside the space shuttle. This US spacecraft carried many pieces of the station to orbit. Modules had to withstand stress from launch. To reach orbit, the space shuttle accelerates from zero to 17,500 miles per hour (28,000 km/h). The acceleration creates extreme loads on the shuttle and its cargo. Once in space, modules needed to be strong enough to hold their air pressure against the vacuum of space outside. Engineers designed cylinder-shaped modules. This shape would fit efficiently inside the space shuttle. It would also

The shuttle's huge cargo bay allowed it to carry large modules to the ISS.

distribute air pressure evenly around the modules' curved sides.

BOT ON BOARD

Robots do difficult, dangerous, or repetitive jobs. Researchers from NASA and private companies built one to help ISS astronauts. Robonaut 2 (R2) looks like a human. It has been on the ISS since 2011. Astronauts are testing how R2 performs in space. They observe how microgravity affects the way R2 works. They watch how skillfully the robot can complete tasks. Researchers hope that someday R2 will provide medical help on the station. In the future, R2 might perform experiments, go on spacewalks, and repair equipment.

The Integrated Truss Structure (ITS) uses carefully selected shapes in its design. The ITS acts as the backbone of the space station. Engineers chose triangle shapes for added strength. Triangles can hold heavy loads. The strong truss can endure the turning of the solar arrays and radiators. It can also support batteries, pumps, and other equipment attached to it.

The solar arrays are flat and wide. With such a large surface area, they collect lots of energy from the sun. The sunlight is converted into electricity. This power is stored in batteries.

SPACE DEBRIS

Spacecraft sometimes create space debris. Old satellites break down and drift in orbit. Tools and equipment accidentally float away during space walks. Even tiny flecks of paint that fall off a rocket can become dangerous at orbital speeds. The chances of a collision are low. But the consequences are serious. A piece of space debris could easily put a hole in the ISS. This would endanger the lives of the astronauts. The US government tracks thousands of pieces of debris in orbit. Sometimes, astronauts must steer the ISS out of the way.

The ISS needed a protective shield in case of a debris strike. Engineers constructed the ISS modules' outer shells from aluminum. The light aluminum is

PARTS OF THE ISS

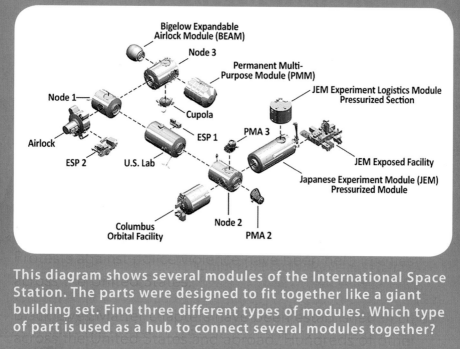

This diagram shows several modules of the International Space Station. The parts were designed to fit together like a giant building set. Find three different types of modules. Which type of part is used as a hub to connect several modules together?

protected by layers of impact-resistant materials such as Kevlar and Nextel. Kevlar is the same material used to make bulletproof vests. Nextel is a ceramic material that is also heat resistant. NASA engineers created a super-tough material by weaving together Kevlar and Nextel. The result is called a Stuffed Whipple Shield. It can stop small debris from putting holes in the station.

TEMPERATURE CONTROL

To protect against extreme temperatures, the ISS is covered in multilayer insulation (MLI). The MLI is made from aluminum-coated Mylar and Dacron. These artificial materials help regulate temperature. The shiny surface of the MLI reflects heat from the sun.

Heat is also generated inside the ISS. Machines are constantly running and making heat. Systems circulate cold water around equipment to keep it cool. The heat is passed to radiators outside the ISS. There, the heat is lost to space.

The windows on the ISS are made from four thick panes of glass. One module, known as the Cupola, has seven windows. It offers the best views on the station. Aluminum shutters protect its windows when the Cupola is not being used. The astronauts use the Cupola to take photographs of Earth and space.

The Cupola is a popular place for astronauts to hang out on the ISS.

LIFE SUPPORT

To survive in space, astronauts need a steady supply of air and water. To provide these, engineers developed life support systems. Most of the station's oxygen is made from water. Electricity from the solar panels is used to split water molecules. The result is oxygen gas. This oxygen is released into the modules. Extra oxygen is kept in storage tanks. Filters remove unhealthy gases and chemicals.

The space station's water supply comes from two sources. Some is brought to the station in containers that look like duffle bags. But water is heavy. Carrying it to the ISS is extremely expensive. Engineers also designed a water recovery system (WRS). The WRS collects and recycles wastewater. Humidity from the air, wash water, and even urine are recycled. This wastewater is filtered several times. Filtering removes things such as hair and lint. The water is then processed to remove chemicals and kill bacteria and viruses. Then it is safe to drink.

POWERING THE ISS

The ISS is powered by four sets of solar arrays. The arrays can generate up to 120 kilowatts of electricity. This is enough electricity to power more than 40 houses.

ENCOURAGING SOCIAL INTERACTION

British space architect David Nixon helped design the ISS. He knew that astronauts spent much of their time working. Nixon believed that the station's equipment should help bring astronauts together. But with limited space, items in the ISS must be compact and practical. Nixon invented the Space Station Wardroom Table. The round table has surfaces that flip up and down. It can be arranged in different ways. It gives astronauts a place to sit, relax, eat, and spend time together. The table folds up and out of the way when it's not being used.

Extra power is stored in batteries. The ISS spends half of its time in shadow, with Earth blocking the sun. When the arrays are shaded, they do not make power. During those times, the ISS uses battery power.

STAYING HAPPY AND HEALTHY

Staying mentally and physically fit in space is hard. Astronauts live for months in cramped conditions. They are

The station's solar arrays tilt toward the sun to maximize the power they generate.

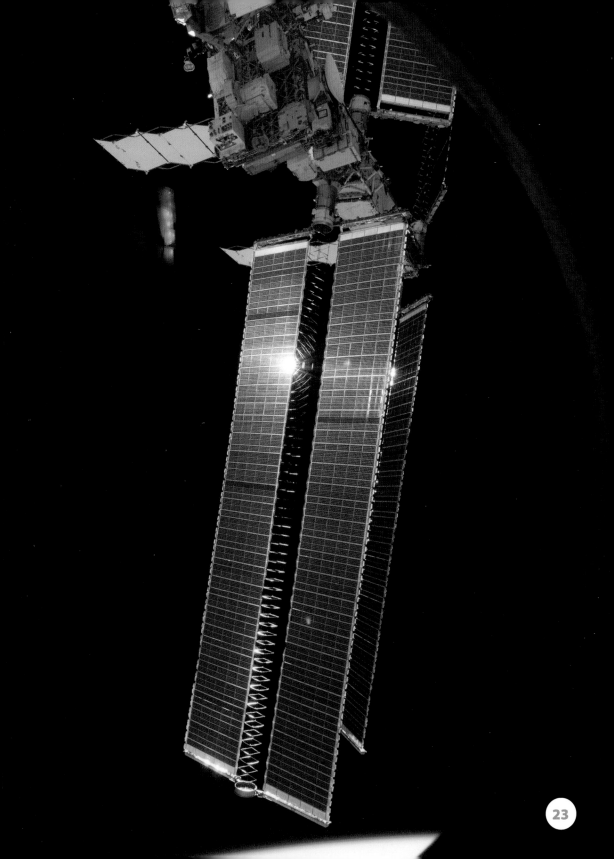

far from family and friends. Every day is scheduled with experiments and other work. Astronauts' sleeping patterns change. They might feel isolated and depressed.

Windows on the ISS give the crew a view of Earth and space. Seeing outside the station helps the crew stay connected to the world. Private areas are also important. Astronauts each have a place to sleep and keep their belongings. They use laptop computers to chat with friends and family back home.

THE EFFECTS OF MICROGRAVITY

Microgravity has negative effects on the human body. It disrupts normal blood flow. On Earth, gravity pulls blood toward a person's feet. In space, blood flows upward into an astronaut's chest and head. This makes blood pressure rise. Astronauts' muscles are also affected. Muscles need gravity to work against. Without gravity, muscles weaken and waste away. In space, astronauts' bodies also lose calcium and phosphorus.

These minerals are needed to make bones strong. Astronauts who stay in space for six months can lose 10 percent of their bone mass.

To keep astronauts healthy, engineers developed special exercise equipment. A treadmill includes straps to hold the astronauts down. Otherwise they would simply float away. A weight-lifting machine includes a platform for them to press their feet against. Astronauts exercise approximately two hours every day. They have checkups to monitor how they are doing.

EXPLORE ONLINE

Chapter Two discusses different parts of the ISS. Go to the website below to read more information about its solar arrays. What new information did you learn from the website? How is the information from the website similar to the information in Chapter Two?

NASA: SOLAR ARRAYS
abdocorelibrary.com/engineering-international-space-station

CHAPTER THREE

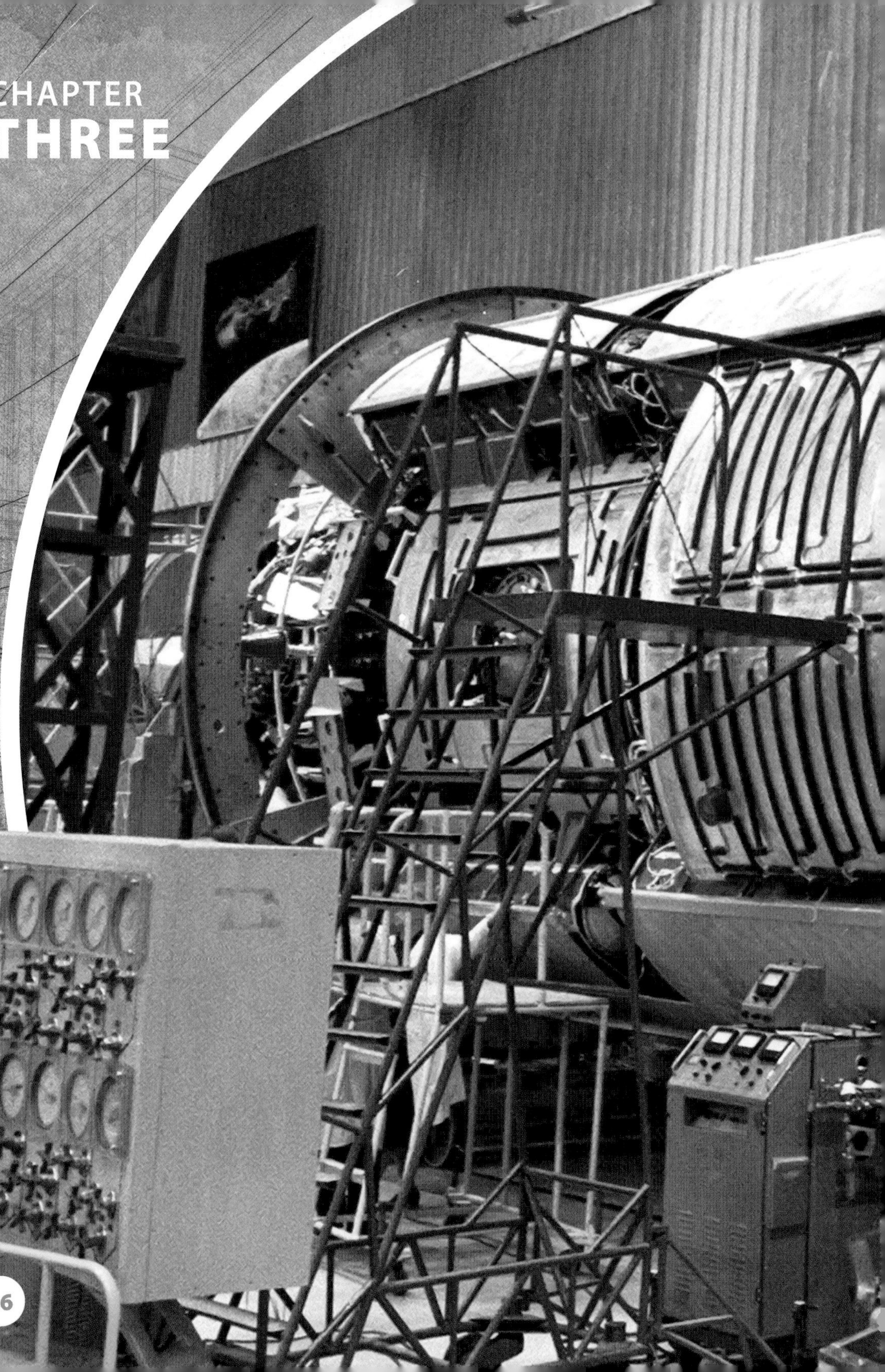

ASSEMBLING
THE ISS

In December 1994, Russian engineers began constructing the Zarya module on Earth. Zarya is named for the Russian word meaning "sunrise." Engineers equipped it with solar panels, batteries, and guidance systems. It would help power the ISS. The first ISS section built by the United States was the Unity module. It is a connecting module, or node. Unity has six areas where other modules can connect. There are more than 50,000 parts inside Unity, including 216 pipes and tubes that transport fluids.

Building the space station began with the construction of the Zarya module on Earth.

US engineers developed an assembly plan. The process would take many years. The pressurized modules had living areas, laboratories, and storage areas. Nodes would link modules together. The ITS would form the backbone of the station. Solar arrays, radiators, a robotic arm, and platforms were added to this core. The platforms would let astronauts work outside the ISS. Docking ports would be connected to the structure. They would provide places where spacecraft could attach to the ISS.

SPACE SUITS

Astronauts wear many types of suits. The white Extravehicular Mobility Unit (EMU) is used for spacewalks. EMUs have several parts. On the helmet, a thin layer of gold keeps out harmful rays from the sun. The upper part of the EMU covers the chest. It is made of hard fiberglass. It contains tubes that carry water and oxygen. The suit's lower part goes over the legs and feet. EMUs have many layers of material. The layers protect astronauts from extreme temperatures, debris, and other dangers. Suits also provide astronauts with oxygen and water during space walks.

CONSTRUCTION BEGINS

Once Zarya and Unity were completed, assembly began. It was time to launch the first pieces of the ISS. Mission 1 took place on November 20, 1998. The Russians launched Zarya into low Earth orbit (LEO). LEO is between 124 miles (200 km) and 1,240 miles (2,000 km) above the Earth. The ISS orbits at about 220 miles (354 km).

No astronauts were inside Zarya when it launched. Once in orbit, Zarya's computer set up the module's antennae, docking ports, and two solar arrays. Zarya was ready to begin its long stay in space.

Two weeks later, the space shuttle *Endeavour* met Zarya. *Endeavour* carried six astronauts. It had the Unity module in its cargo bay. On board *Endeavour*, astronaut Nancy Currie operated a robotic arm. She used the arm to remove the Unity module from the cargo bay. Then she latched the module onto Zarya. During the 12-day mission, the crew performed three EVAs. They added

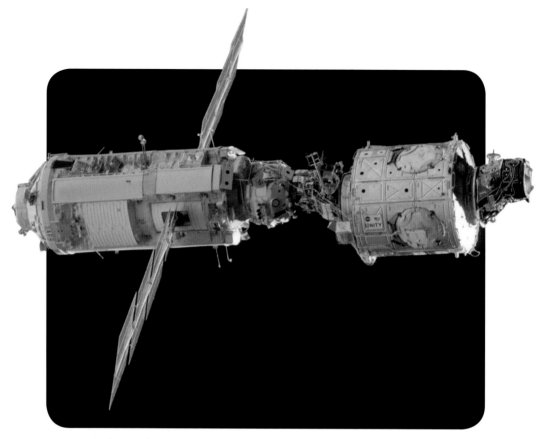

Zarya, *left*, and Unity, *right*, linked up in December 1998.

cables and installed equipment on both modules. *Endeavour*'s crew returned to Earth. The station was still not ready for people. But the mission ensured that both modules were ready for the next phase.

THE ISS GROWS

The next two missions took place in May 1999 and May 2000. Space shuttle crews brought supplies and equipment to the ISS. They prepared the ISS to receive the Russian Zvezda module. Zvezda launched on July 12, 2000. It docked with the station a few weeks later. Zvezda contains living areas. It also has life support, data processing, and communications systems. Flight controllers on Earth use the communications system to remotely command the ISS. Zvezda has a docking port where spacecraft and European ATVs can attach. The ATV is a delivery craft. Each one can carry 16,903 pounds (7,667 kg) of food, water, air, and other supplies. In September and October 2000, two more crews visited the ISS. They delivered supplies and did maintenance work. They also installed a truss section.

EXPEDITION 1

On October 31, 2000, the Expedition 1 mission launched on a Russian rocket. The crew included two Russians and one American. They were the first people to live and work on the ISS. They activated computers, life support, and other systems. They also began several experiments. The crew helped install the US Destiny module. This structure is a scientific laboratory.

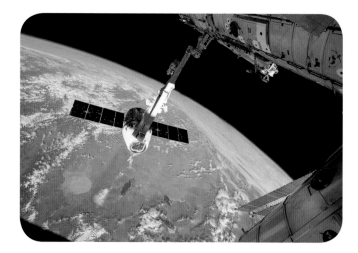

Canadarm2 allows the station's crew to grab incoming cargo vessels and line them up for a safe docking.

They also added more truss structures and solar arrays. The crew returned to Earth in February 2001.

Canadarm2 was installed in April 2001. Constructed by the Canadians, this robotic arm is an important helper. It travels along the station's trusses. Canadarm2 latches onto modules, making it easier to install them. It lugs bulky equipment back and forth. It even moves astronauts during space walks. Crews used Canadarm2 to help build the rest of the ISS.

COMPLETION OF THE ISS

Piece by piece, the ISS grew over the next ten years. In 2008 Japan contributed a laboratory module named

Kibo. More truss sections were installed, along with solar arrays and radiators. The ESA's Columbus laboratory module was added. Inside Columbus, astronauts experiment with cells, tissues, plants, and insects. They study how liquids and metals behave in microgravity. They make discoveries that can improve life on Earth. Italy built a cargo-carrying spacecraft called Leonardo. It carried supplies to the

PERSPECTIVES

PERSPECTIVES
DISASTER HALTS ISS PROGRESS

On February 1, 2003, the space shuttle *Columbia* fell apart as it was returning to Earth. The spacecraft's heat shield had failed. All seven crew members died. After the disaster, NASA grounded the space shuttles. It investigated the accident. Without shuttles, ISS construction also came to a halt. The crew already on the ISS extended their stay. They were greatly saddened by the loss of their friends. But they remained positive. They felt it was important to keep the ISS going. The ISS crew later returned to Earth on a Russian spacecraft. Space shuttles did not return to flight until July 26, 2005.

ISS CONSTRUCTION
TIMELINE

The ISS was constructed over the course of many years, with components delivered by several nations using a variety of spacecraft. This timeline highlights the major additions to the station. What complications might construction in space bring? Are there any ways in which it might be easier than construction on Earth?

1998: Russia launches the Zarya module. The United States launches the Unity module.

2000: Russia launches the Zvezda module. The United States launches the Z-1 and P-6 trusses.

2001: The United States launches the Destiny module and an airlock. Russia launches the Pirs docking compartment.

2002: The United States launches the S-1 truss, the P-1 truss, and solar arrays.

2006: The United States launches the P-3, P-4, and P-5 trusses and solar arrays.

2007: The United States launches the S-3, S-4, and S-5 trusses, solar arrays, and the Harmony module.

2008: The United States launches the Columbus and Kibo laboratories.

2009: The United States launches the S-6 truss and solar arrays.

2010: The United States launches the Tranquility and Cupola modules.

2011: The United States launches the Leonardo module.

2016: The United States launches the Bigelow Expandable Activity Module.

station several times. In 2011 it was added to the ISS permanently as a storage area.

NASA's space shuttles were retired in 2011. They had been the main way to launch and assemble US parts of the ISS. Major construction was now complete. Within two decades, the ISS had gone from an idea on paper to a working space station. Ever since Expedition 1 in October 2000, people have been continually living in space aboard the ISS.

FURTHER EVIDENCE

Chapter Three discusses how the ISS was constructed in space. Review the chapter and identify one of its main points. What key evidence supports this point? Go to the website below and explore more ideas about the ISS. Find a quote from the website that supports this point.

NATIONAL GEOGRAPHIC: INTERNATIONAL SPACE STATION

abdocorelibrary.com/engineering-international-space-station

CHAPTER FOUR

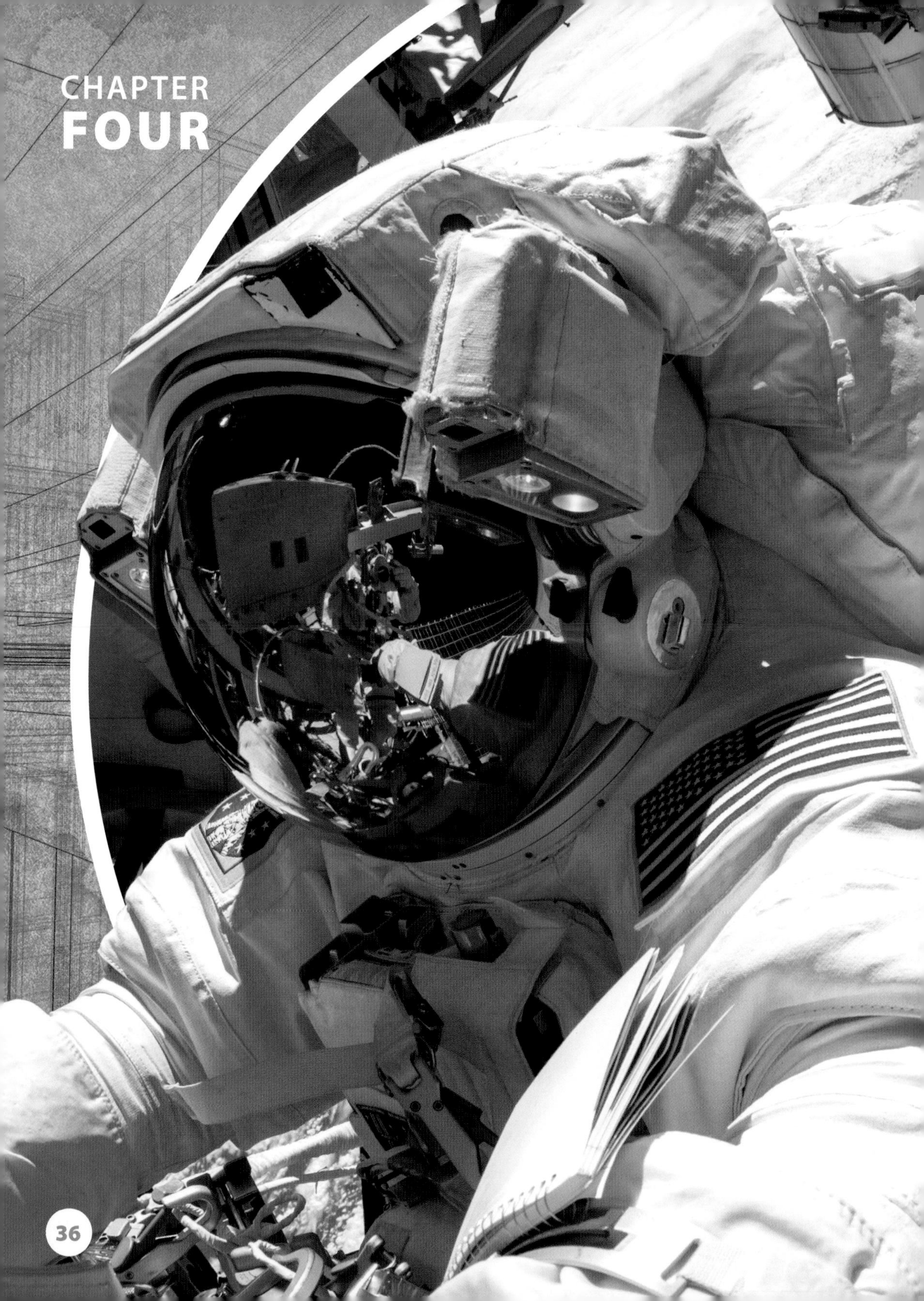

THE ISS TODAY

The ISS remains active 24 hours a day, seven days a week. People all over the globe work to keep the crew healthy and safe. Staff at control centers in Houston, Texas, and Korolev, Russia, coordinate all ISS operations. Over the years, more equipment came to the ISS. New control centers were set up in France, Canada, Germany, and other locations to handle the extra work.

By 2018 astronauts had made more than 50 expeditions to the ISS. Crews stay for an average of six months. They update equipment inside and outside the ISS.

People have been living and working at the ISS continuously for more than 15 years.

COMMERCIAL CREW PROGRAM

After NASA retired the space shuttles in 2011, it began using Russian rockets to transport astronauts. But it had new plans on the horizon. The Commercial Crew Program aims to launch astronauts on US rockets again. It involves partnerships with companies. These companies work with NASA to design new spacecraft. The company Boeing is building a spacecraft called the CST-100 Starliner. The company SpaceX is developing one called Dragon. Early versions of Dragon have already carried cargo to the ISS.

The station's astronauts have completed more than 200 space walks. Inside they have conducted more than 1,000 experiments.

Astronauts are always learning and teaching. NASA challenges students to design experiments for the ISS. Astronauts often talk to students about their life and work in space. When they are not working, astronauts exercise and

By learning how to live and work in space, astronauts on the ISS are paving the way for future space expeditions.

relax. They contact family and friends on Earth using e-mail.

EXPLORING DEEP SPACE

The ISS continues to provide a wealth of information about space. It helps scientists understand what humans will need for long-term survival in space. Technologies developed for the ISS are being used to design new spacecraft.

In the future, deep space missions will go to the moon, to Mars, and beyond. Astronauts will need to live in space for months or years at a time. The experience gained on the ISS will make this possible.

SPACE SPINOFFS

Research done on the ISS has resulted in new technologies. Some technologies become products that benefit people on Earth. These are called space spinoffs. One technology developed on the ISS transmits medical images over long distances. This helps patients get medical treatment when they are far from a hospital. Other spinoffs include a water recycling system and air-cleaning devices.

STRAIGHT TO THE
SOURCE

A company called Bigelow Aerospace designed a module that inflates in space. Journalist Kenneth Chang described the module:

> Instead of metal, its walls will be made of floppy cloth, making it easier to launch (and then inflate). . . . The soft sides of the module, called the Bigelow Expandable Activity Module, or BEAM, will allow it to be scrunched like a T-shirt in a suitcase.
>
> At the space station, it will be attached to an air lock and then inflated like a balloon and expanded by a factor of 10 to its full size. . . . [The] structure is carefully designed not to pop. The fabric walls will consist of several layers including Vectran, a bullet-resistant material. Even if punctured by a high-speed meteorite, the fabric does not tear.

Source: Kenneth Chang. "For Space Station, a Pod That Folds Like a Shirt and Inflates Like a Balloon." *New York Times*. New York Times, January 16, 2013. Web. Accessed May 29, 2017.

Back It Up
The author discusses several advantages of the inflatable module. Based on this passage and what you have read in this book, what are these advantages?

FAST FACTS

- Space stations allow astronauts to live and work in space for long periods.

- The United States, Russia, Canada, Japan, and other nations partnered to build the ISS.

- The ISS is the largest structure ever built in space.

- The ISS includes modules, nodes, trusses, and solar arrays.

- The first parts of the ISS were launched in 1998.

- The ISS was assembled in space.

- The ISS serves as a huge laboratory for scientific research.

- The ISS is built of aluminum, which is light but strong.

- Human-made materials such as Kevlar, Mylar, and Dacron protect the modules.

- Solar arrays collect the sun's energy and convert it to electricity to power the ISS.

- Staff at Mission Control Centers around the world monitor the ISS.

- Building the ISS and working on the station have taught engineers and astronauts a great deal about what it will take to live in deep space on future missions.

STOP AND
THINK

Tell the Tale

Chapter Two discusses some of the challenges astronauts on the ISS might encounter in space. Imagine you are an astronaut on the ISS. Write 200 words about some of the difficulties you experience on your mission.

Surprise Me

Chapter Three discusses the assembly of the ISS in space. After reading this book, what two or three facts about the ISS did you find most surprising? Write a few sentences about each fact. Why did you find each fact surprising?

Another View

This book talks about the design and construction of the ISS. As you know, every source is different. Ask an adult to help you find another source about this subject. Write a short essay comparing and contrasting the new source's point of view with that of this book's author. What is the point of view of each author? How are they similar and why? How are they different and why?

Why Do I Care?

Maybe you are not interested in exploring space. But that doesn't mean you can't think about ways space exploration benefits people on Earth. In what ways has space exploration affected your life? How might it benefit other people?

GLOSSARY

airlock
a sealed compartment with two sets of doors that is used to travel from a spacecraft into space and back

array
a group of items that form a complete unit

atmosphere
the layer of air that surrounds Earth

cosmonaut
a Russian astronaut

debris
pieces of waste

dock
to join two spacecraft together

microgravity
the weightless condition experienced in orbit

module
a self-contained unit of a spacecraft

node
a spacecraft module that connects to other modules or parts

orbit
to travel around another object in a regular pattern

solar
having to do with the sun

truss
a support structure to which parts are connected

ONLINE
RESOURCES

To learn more about the International Space Station, visit our free resource websites below.

Core Library
CONNECTION
FREE! COMMON CORE MULTIMEDIA RESOURCES

Visit **abdocorelibrary.com** for free Common Core resources for teachers and students, including vetted activities, multimedia, and booklinks, for deeper subject comprehension.

Booklinks
NONFICTION NETWORK
FREE! ONLINE NONFICTION RESOURCES

Visit **abdobooklinks.com** for free additional online weblinks for further learning. These links are routinely monitored and updated to provide the most current information available.

LEARN
MORE

Gagne, Tammy. *Women in Earth and Space Exploration.* Minneapolis, MN: Abdo Publishing, 2017.

Space: Visual Encyclopedia. New York: DK Publishing, 2016.

INDEX

About the Author

Cecilia Pinto McCarthy has written several nonfiction books for young readers. When she is not writing, she enjoys teaching ecology classes at a nature sanctuary. She lives with her family north of Boston, Massachusetts.